Water Power

Louis Capra

What helps crops grow?

3

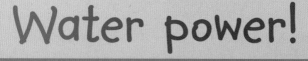

Water power!

Farmers use water to grow crops.

What helps fight fires?

6

7

Water power!

Firefighters spray water on fires to put them out.

What helps make a canyon?

Water power!

Water rushing through a canyon wears away its rocky sides.

What helps light cities?

15

Water power!

Water falling from a dam can be used to make electricity to light cities.

What helps make beaches?

Water power!

Ocean waves carry sand and leave it on beaches.

What helps keep you clean?

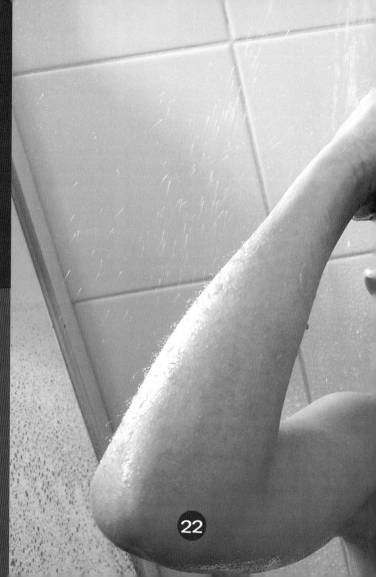

22

Water power!

Index